- Stitch 3" (7.5 cm) Color B center corners to each end of the remaining two 5" (12.5 cm) Color E sashing strips.

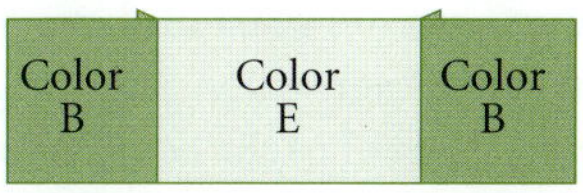

- Stitch these strips to the center block.

- Stitch a Color C right triangle to each side of the pieced center block.

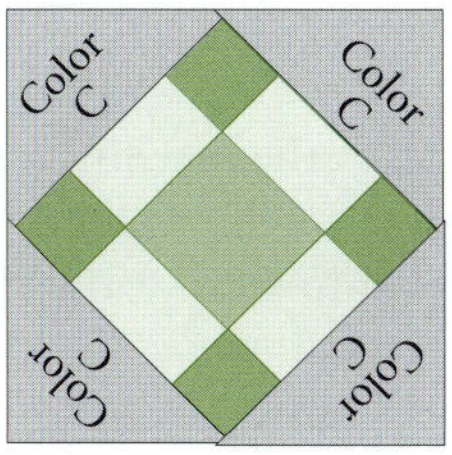

- Stitch two of the 3" x 13¾" (7.5 cm x 35 cm) Color E sashing strips to the pieced block.

- Stitch a 3" (7.5 cm) Color D corner square to each end of the remaining two Color E sashing strips.

- Stitch these strips to the pieced pillow top.

- A [illegible] ti[illegible] pa[illegible] from the Amazing Designs® "Nature's Reflections" Memory Card.

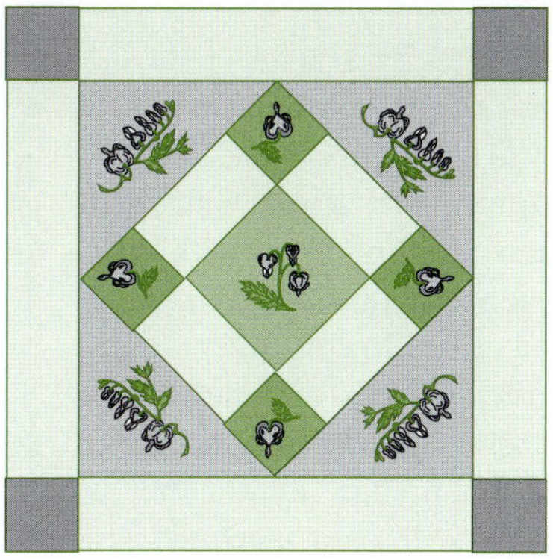

- Optional: Add piping to the outer edge of the pillow top.
  - Join short edges of piping strips to form a continuous strip. Joining strips on the bias helps reduce bulk.

  - Fold strip in half, meeting lengthwise edges.

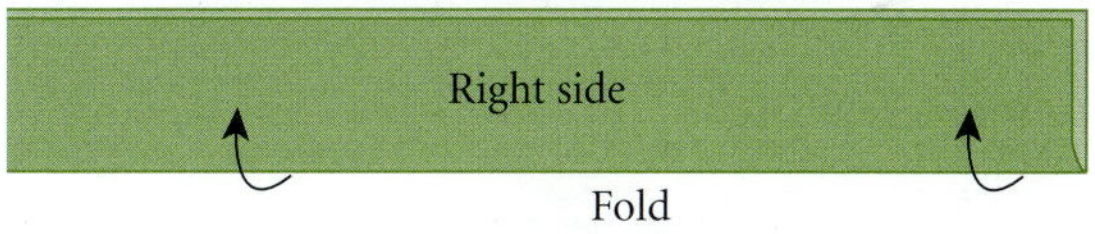

  - Position piping on right side of pillow, beginning in the middle of one side, meeting cut edges. Overlap ends of piping, angling piping to outer edge. Machine baste in place.

- Prepare pillow back using your favorite technique.
- Join front to back, right sides together. Turn pillow right side out.

Purchasing Machine Embroidery Designs

Embroidery designs are available on several types of media: memory cards, floppy disks, and CDs. There are differences in how you use each and whether you need additional equipment.

1. Memory Card
   - A memory card fits directly into a slot in the sewing machine.
   - A memory card doesn't need a computer to interact with the sewing machine; it uses the sewing machine's built-in computer.
   - A memory card is designed for a specific brand of sewing machine. Be sure to purchase a card that is compatible with your machine.

2. Computer disk (Floppy disk)
   - A floppy disk requires a separate home computer with a floppy disk drive and a software program designed specifically for your sewing machine.
   - Some brands of sewing machines, such as Pfaff, have software that allows you to transfer a design directly from a disk inserted in the computer to the sewing machine. Others require you to use a reader/writer box designed specifically for that machine to make the transfer from computer to sewing machine.

3. CD
   - A CD also requires a separate home computer with a CD ROM drive and a software program specifically for the sewing machine.
   - The way a CD works is similar to the way a computer disk works, except a CD holds more information.

Setting up for Machine Embroidery

Each brand of sewing machine has specific instructions for attaching the embroidery unit and getting ready to embroider. For example, my Pfaff machine tells me to turn off the machine, attach the embroidery unit, and then turn the machine back on. Check your owner's manual for specific instructions for your machine.

1. Machine setup:
   - Lower the feed dogs.
   - Insert a machine embroidery needle compatible with the type of thread used for the embroidery. For example, use a conventional Machine Embroidery Needle with rayon machine embroidery thread, and a Metallic Machine Embroidery Needle with metallic threads. Machine Embroidery Needles feature a specially designed needle scarf and eye to virtually eliminate thread breakage when stitching dense embroidery designs, while Metallic Machine Embroidery Needles feature a fine shaft and sharp point to eliminate thread breakage, a specialized scarf to prevent skipped stitches, and an elongated eye to prevent thread-stripping.

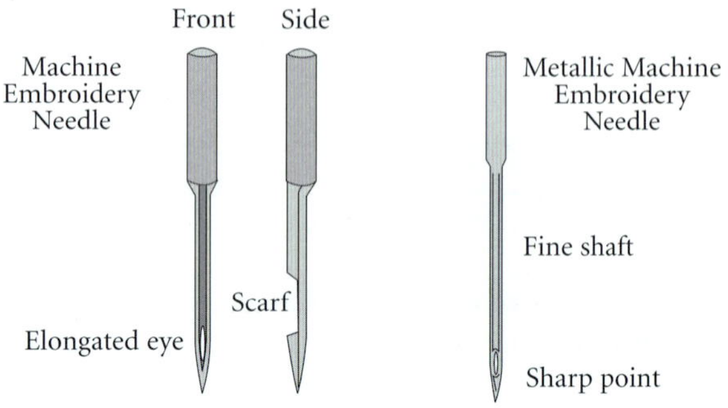

   - Thread the top of the machine with machine embroidery thread. Use a lightweight thread such as Madeira Bobbinfil or Cotton Prewound Bobbins in the bobbin.
   - Loosen the top tension by two numbers or notches.
   - Insert the Memory Card and select the design.

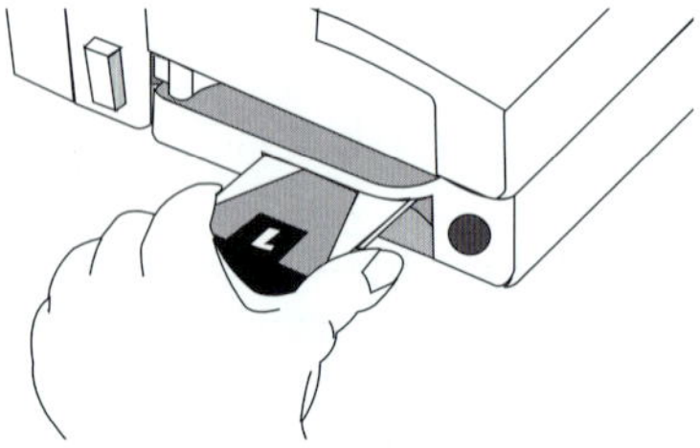

2. Interface the embroidery fabric and/or add stabilizers.

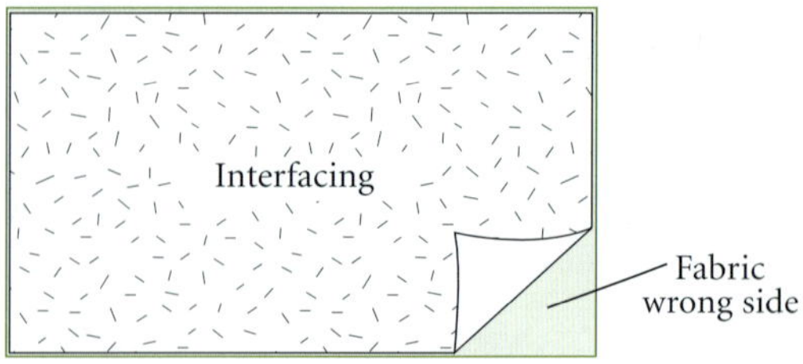

One of the most common problems for beginning embroiderers is using insufficient stabilization. Always test the stitching on a sample before stitching on the actual garment or project to determine the best combination of stabilizers for the fabric and design.

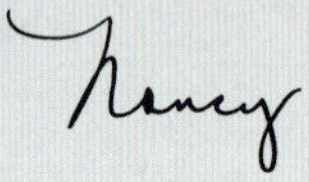

- Add a layer of fusible interfacing. Interfacing prevents the temporary stabilizer from showing through after stitching is completed. Select an interfacing weight compatible with the fabric: Use a lightweight interfacing such as Lightweight Pellon® for lightweight fabrics and a heavier interfacing like Pellon® ShirTailor® for heavier fabrics like denim.
- Add a temporary stabilizer to prevent stitch distortion. This stabilizer is generally removed after stitching is completed. Choose a stabilizer appropriate for the fabric and stitch density.
  - Press-on stabilizer—for example, Totally Stable. Especially suited for knits and loosely woven fabrics.
  - Tear-away stabilizer—for example, Pellon® Stitch-N-Tear®. Ideal for dense stitching where tearing won't distort embroidery stitches or the fabric.
  - Cut-away stabilizer—for example, Soft 'n Sheer™. Appropriate for delicate fabrics and designs which might be distorted by tearing away the stabilizer.
  - Water-soluble stabilizer—for example, Avalon® by Madeira. For use on washable fabrics; easily removed by water, leaving no visible residue.
  - Sticky-backed stabilizer—for example, Filmoplast Stic. Used to stabilize fabric or garment sections too small to be hooped, or fabrics on which a hoop might leave an unsightly impression.

3. Position the design on the fabric.
   - Ensuring an embroidery design will be stitched precisely where you want it is one of the biggest concerns in machine embroidery. Here are three ways of helping properly position the design.
     - Stitch out the design on a test fabric. Trace around the inside of the hoop before removing the fabric from the hoop. Also mark horizontal and vertical center marks and the top of the design. Cut around the traced line and use that section as a placement guide, positioning it on the embroidery fabric.

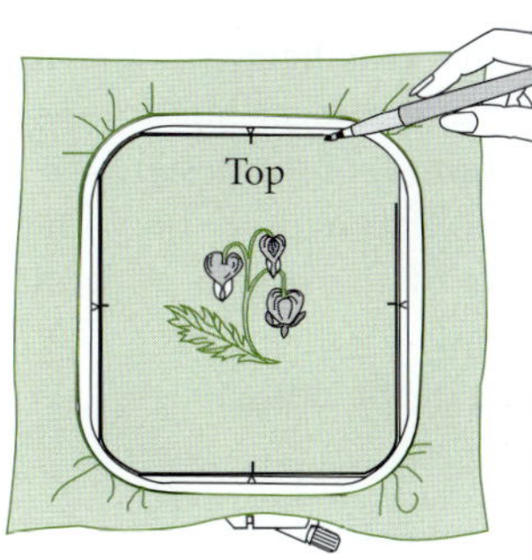

Trace inside of hoop

Cut along marked lines

     - Use a purchased template. These templates have a crosshatch with positioning holes as well as a center hole, making it easy to precisely position the design in the hoop. Tape the template in place with Sewer's Fix-it Tape before hooping the fabric; remove the template after positioning the machine needle for the start of the design.

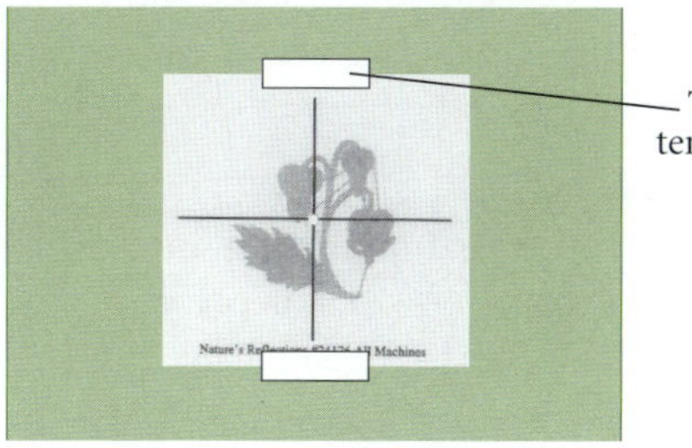

Tape template

     - Use the trace or "walk-about" feature available on some machines. Insert a washable fabric marker in the hole of the embroidery foot. Press the appropriate button on the machine and the machine will trace around the perimeter of the design as well as indicate the center needle position.

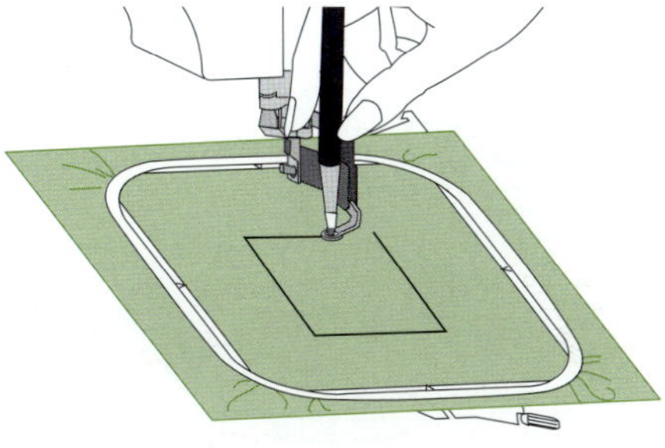

4. Insert the hoop in the machine.
   - Place the outer hoop on a flat surface.
   - Position the fabric over the hoop.

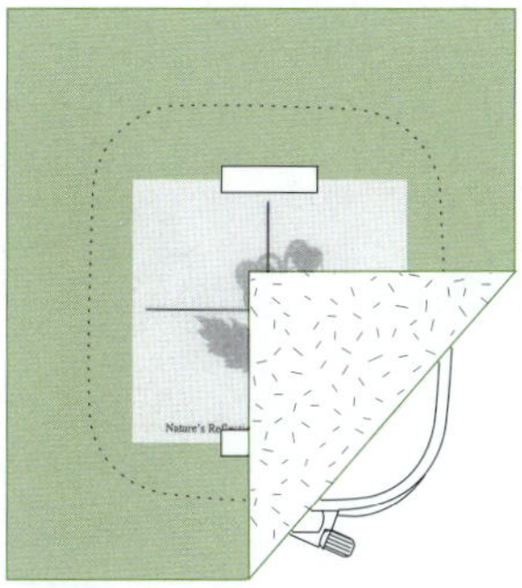

Position fabric over hoop

   - Place the inner hoop over the fabric and press down firmly with the heels of your hands, aligning the cross marks of the design or template with the markings on the hoop.

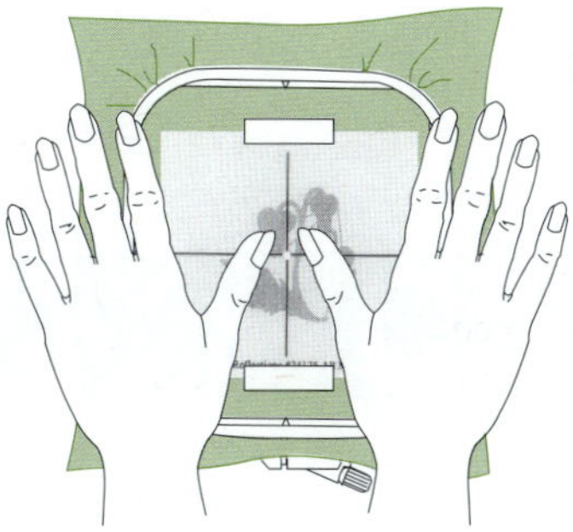

Press outer hoop in place

- Move the needle to the design's starting point.
- Lower the presser foot to ensure the design is properly positioned. Remove any templates prior to stitching.

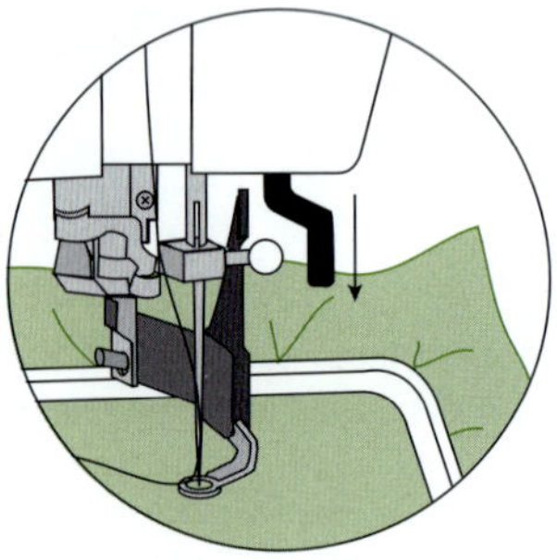

5. Stitch the design.
   - Bring up the bobbin thread; sew a few stitches and clip the thread.

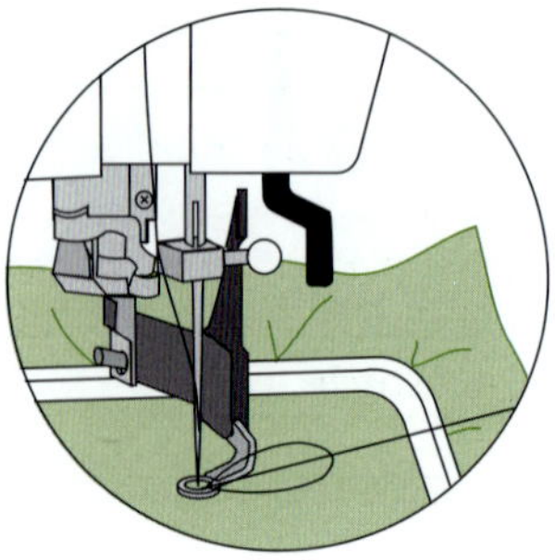

- Stitch the first color.
- To change threads, clip the needle thread at both the needle and the thread spool. Remove the thread by pulling it out through the needle. This flosses the machine tension disks and prevents lint from being drawn into the machine mechanism.

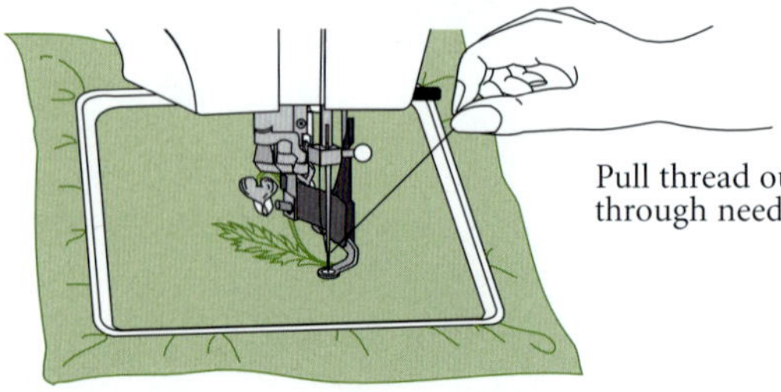

Organize your threads in sequential order before beginning stitching. Line them up in the order they will be stitched to make it easy to move from color to color.

Nancy

Beyond the Basics

Now that you're familiar with embroidery basics, explore other options which allow you to showcase your creativity. You can dramatically expand your library of embroidery designs—and your embroidery options—by using portions of a design, combining designs, or manipulating the design.

That's what Eileen did on this shirt, pictured in color on the back cover, using designs from Amazing Designs® Memory Cards 110 Country Garden, and 101 Floral. By repeating and rotating the bow on the pocket four times and skipping some of the colors in the original design, she created the perfect frame for the French herb motif. Along the lower edge, she stitched several of the herb designs, creating an attractive border.

1. Repeat a design to make a pocket frame.
   - Remove the pocket from the garment.
   - Back the pocket with a piece of cutaway stabilizer large enough to be hooped, adhering the pocket with spray adhesive or by basting.

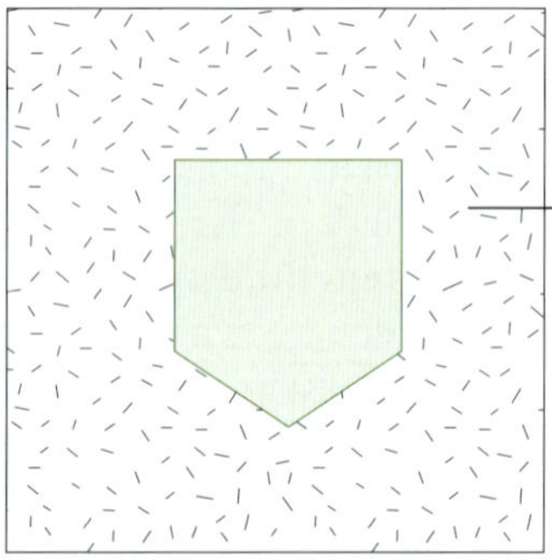

   - Use a template to mark the positions for the embroidery designs. Align the crosshairs on the template with the marks on the embroidery hoop.
   - Determine which portion(s) of the design you wish to use. (In this instance, Eileen used only the bow.) Delete unwanted parts of the design and resave the design with a new name.
   - Stitch out the first part of the design.

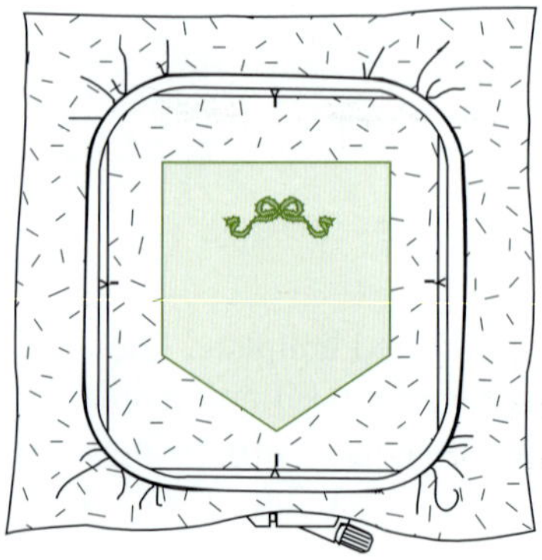

- Rotate the design, using the template to verify positioning. Stitch the second part of the design.

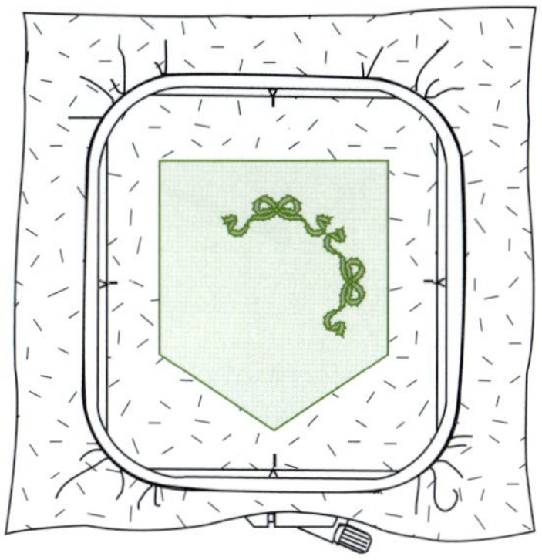

- Repeat, rotating and stitching two additional bows until the entire design has been stitched.

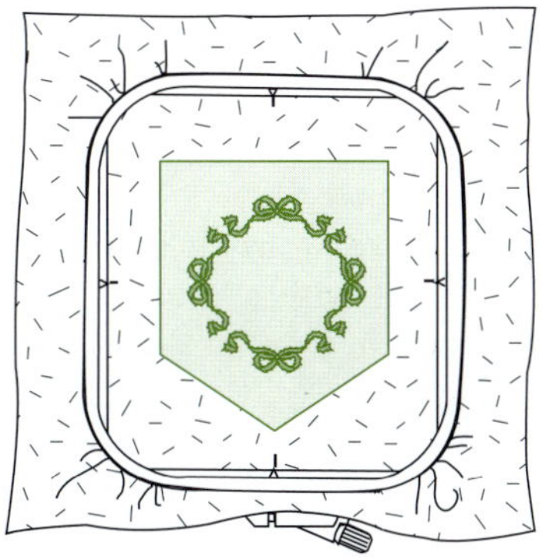

2. Change a design by skipping one or more colors in the design.
   - Bring up the design on the screen of the sewing machine.

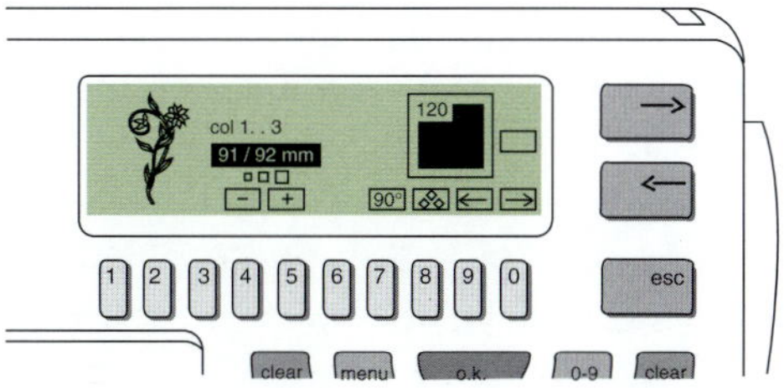

   - Use the "color select" key to move through each of the colors in the design. This identifies both the coloration and the type of stitches for each portion of the design.

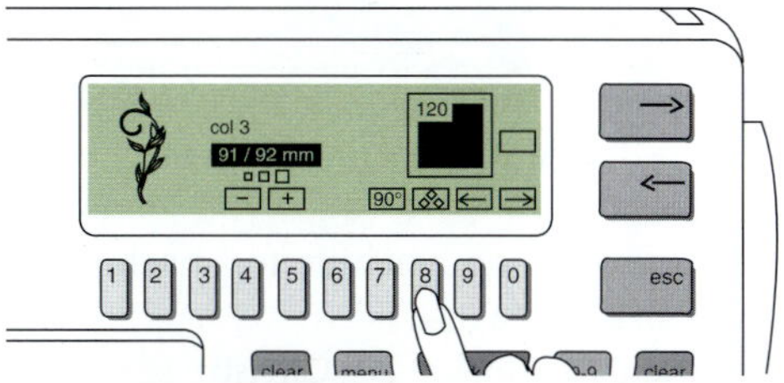

   - Select the portions of the design you wish to use. Eileen used the following design on a pique shell. She used only the design outline, but eliminated the fill stitches.

   - Use the color select key to begin stitching at the desired portion of the design. Repeat, until all desired portions of the design have been stitched.

3. Make attractive stationery and greeting cards by stitching or appliquéing embroidery samples onto paper.
   - Choose a heavier, beefier paper such as card stock, available in a stationery store. Stitching could tear or leave unattractive holes in lighter weight paper.
   - Here are several ways of combining embroidery and paper. Designs pictured below are from Amazing Designs® "Nature's Reflections" Embroidery Card.
     - Insert a sticky-backed stabilizer such as Filmoplast Stic in the hoop. Remove the paper backing, exposing the adhesive. Position the card stock over the adhesive and stitch.

     - Use stitched samples of embroidery designs as appliqués. Back the embroidery with a fusible web and fuse to card stock.

     - Frame the embroidery by fusing it to another fabric. Then fuse that fabric to the card stock.

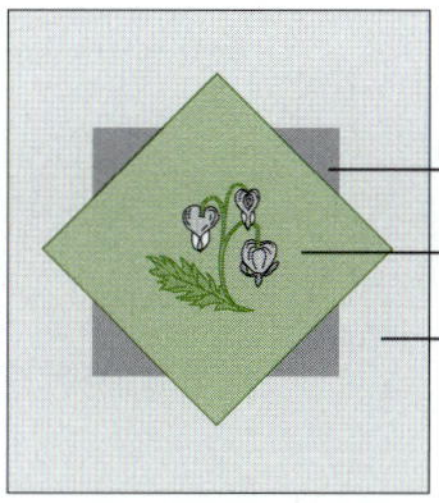

- Embroider a design on organdy or organza, hooping both the fabric and a water soluble stabilizer. After completing stitching, cut out a square or rectangle including the embroidery. Fringe the outer edges of the organdy and position and stitch the embroidery to ribbon. Stitch or glue the ribbon to the card stock.

Combining Embroidery Designs

Next, combine embroidery designs to give added interest to a sewing project. This embroidered tabletop tree skirt can bring back fond memories of Christmas every time you use it. It features a series of proportional embroidery designs combined to create a holiday landscape. Finished diameter: approximately 21½" (54.8 cm).

Supplies needed:

- ⅜ yd. (0.35 m) denim 60" (152.5 cm) wide, or ⅜ yd. (0.35 m) of narrower fabric
- ¾ yd. (0.7 m) Pellon® ShirTailor® fusible interfacing
- ⅝ yd. (0.6 m) red fabric (lining and piping)
- Amazing Designs® "Memories of Christmas" Memory Card
- "Memories of Christmas" Memory Card Templates
- Madeira Rayon Embroidery Threads

Making the Tree Skirt

1. Fuse interfacing to the wrong side of the denim. Interface the entire fabric, not only the embroidery, to provide added support.

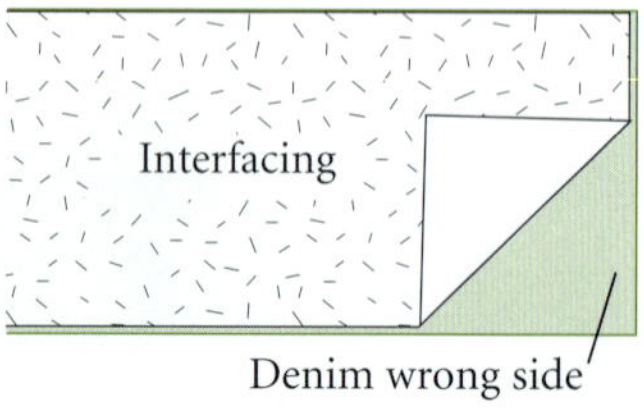

2. Prepare the pattern.
   - Enlarge the half-pattern on page 18 as indicated. Trace the half-pattern onto Grid Grip™ or a plastic quilting template material such as Templar®, allowing room for the second half of the pattern.

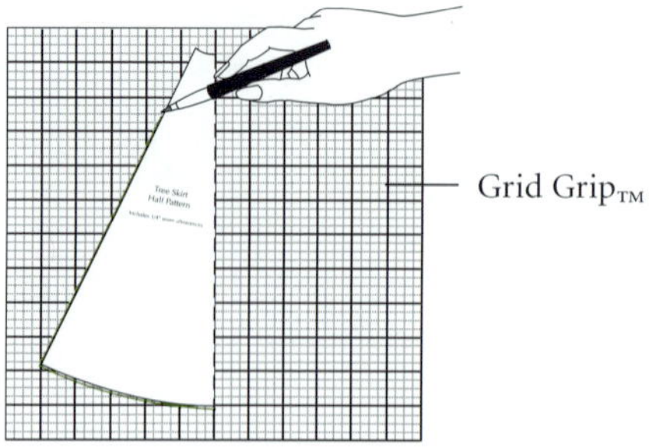

   - With paper, fold along the center line and cut out a complete pattern. With template material, flip the pattern to trace the second half.

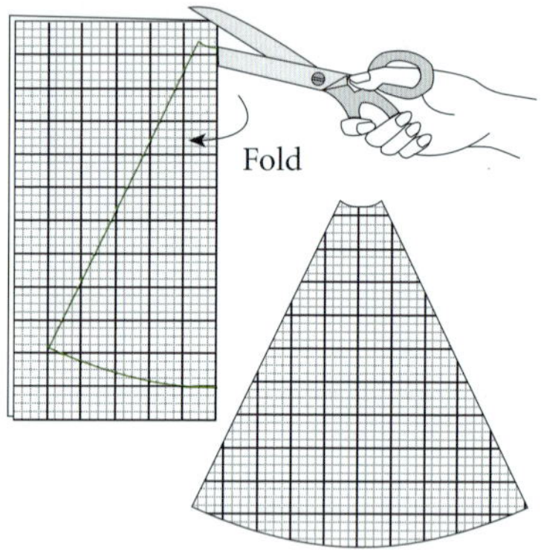

   - Position pattern on the right side of the denim. Using Chaco-Liner or a Chacopel Fine Pencil, outline six wedges. Don't cut out the wedges; it's easier to embroider the designs on a larger piece of fabric before cutting them out.

3. Determine design placements, hoop the fabric, and stitch the designs.
   - Set up the sewing machine for machine embroidery as detailed on page 4.
   - Use the "Memories of Christmas" Memory Card Templates or the stitched out test designs to arrange the designs as desired on the tree skirt, beginning with background sections.

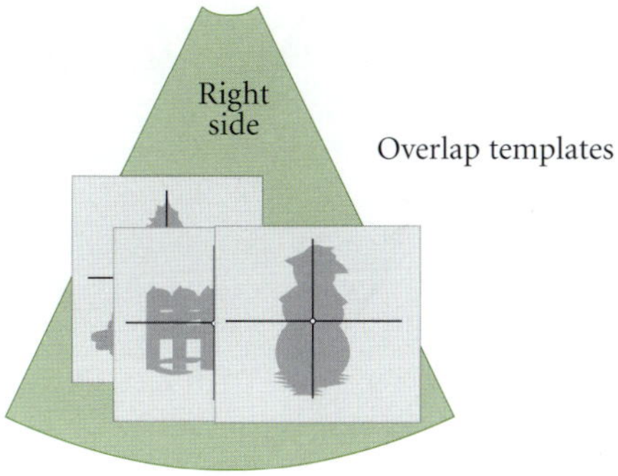

- It's important to determine which designs will be in the background, midground, and foreground before beginning stitching because you can't add embroidery behind embroidery once it's stitched.

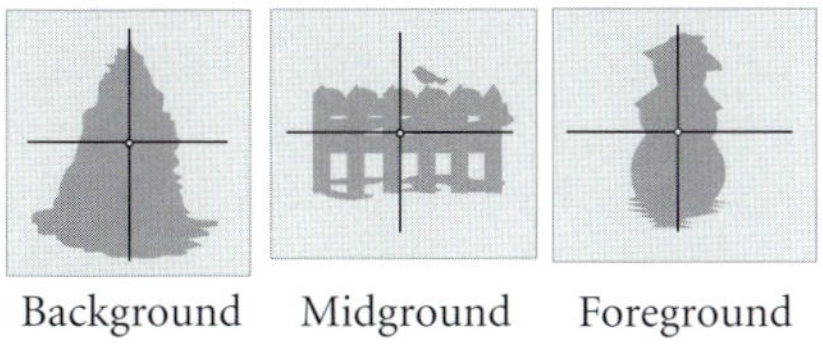

- Position the designs to check that proportion is correct. If two designs are part of the same scene, place the one which is actually the largest in real life in the background to provide a sense of depth and proportion.
- Separate designs in the landscape to make the design more believable.

• Hoop the fabric.
  - Begin with background designs. Use a template as detailed on page 5 to help accurately position the design.
  - With commercial templates, align the cross marks on the template with the marks on the hoop. Tape template in place. Insert the hoop into the embroidery unit, adding a layer of stabilizer under the hoop. Move the needle so it is positioned over the center hole. Then remove the template and stitch the design.

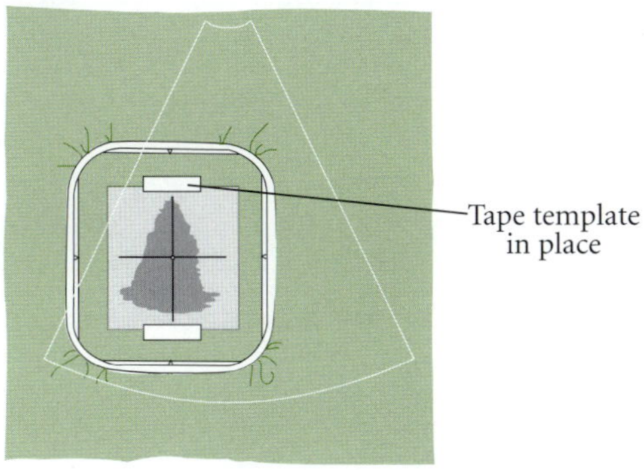

  - With stitched out templates, place the template over the fabric and pin or baste it in place. Hoop the fabric, adding stabilizer under the hoop. If your machine has a "trace" or "walk about" feature, use it to verify design placement. Move the needle to starting position; then remove the template and stitch.

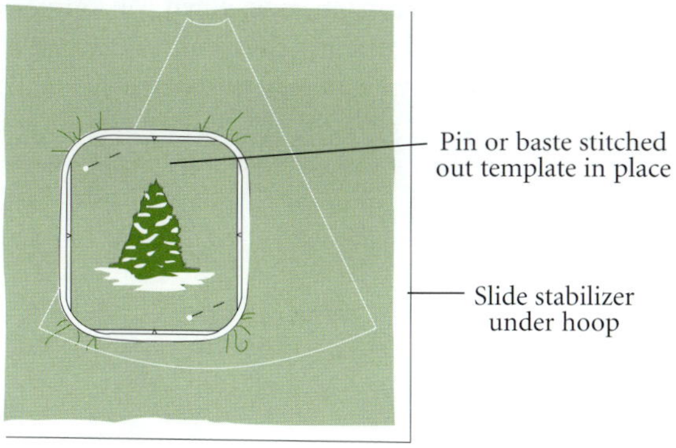

• After stitching the first design, pin or tape the next template in place and repeat the process, working from background to foreground until all designs have been embroidered.

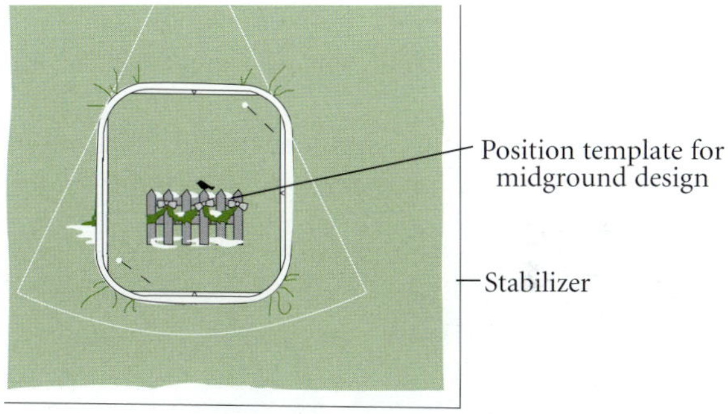

• Lightly press the embroidered sections and cut out the wedges, following traced outlines.

4. Assemble the tree skirt, using ¼" (0.6 cm) seam allowances.
   • Add piping to each seam.
     - Cut three ¾" (2 cm) straight grain strips parallel to one selvage on the lining fabric.
     - Press each strip in half, meeting lengthwise edges, wrong sides together, to form piping.

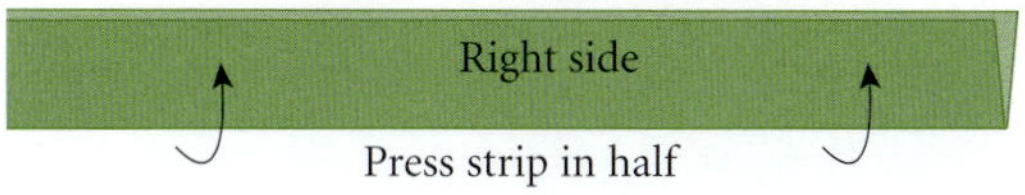

     - Place piping on right side of one wedge, along side edge, meeting cut edges.
     - Meet a second wedge to the first wedge, right sides together, meeting cut edges.
     - Stitch, joining the two wedges, with piping sandwiched in between.

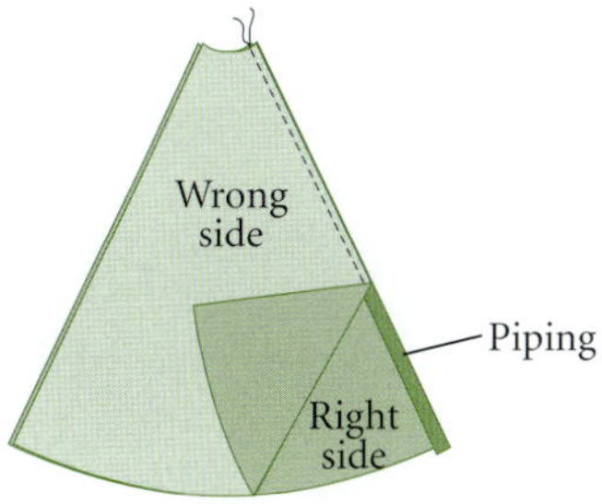

- Press seam flat, then to one side.
- Repeat until all wedges have been joined.

• Place tree skirt, right side down, on one end of the lining. Cut lining using the denim skirt as the pattern.

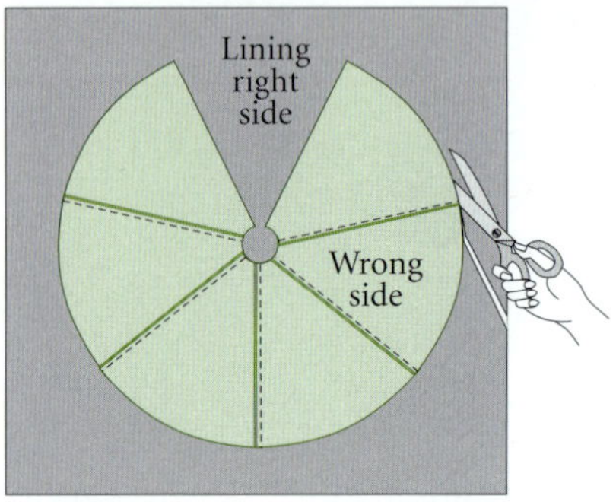

• Add piping to outer edges of tree skirt.
  - From remaining lining fabric, cut ¾" (2 cm) bias strips. Seam strips to form one continuous strip approximately 90" (229 cm) long.
  - Press bias in half, wrong sides together, meeting lengthwise edges.
  - Baste piping to right side of tree skirt outer edges as shown. Do not add piping to inner center circle of tree skirt.

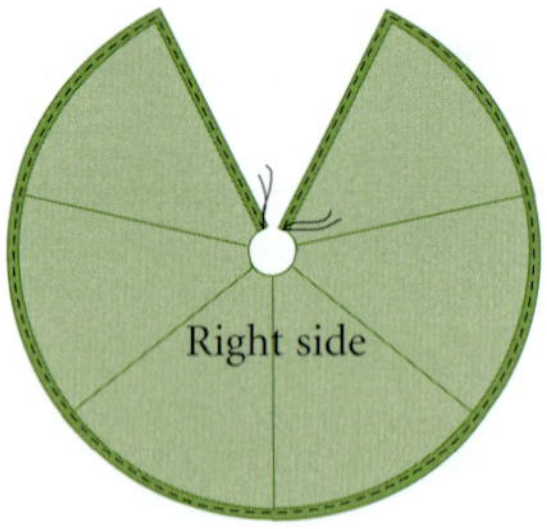

• Add ties to the inner edge.
  - Cut two 1" x 9" (2.5 cm x 23 cm) straight strips from the lining fabric.
  - Meet lengthwise edges, right sides together; stitch a ¼" (0.6 cm) seam, creating a tube.

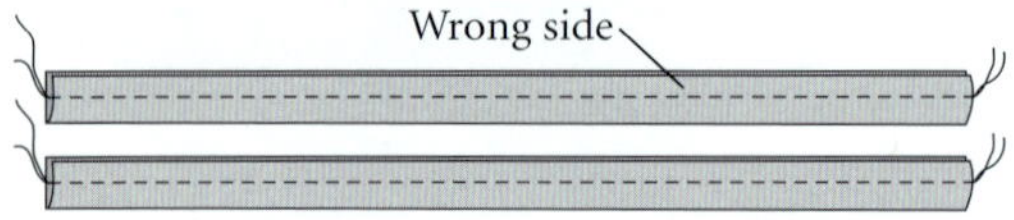

  - Turn tube right side out using Fasturn®. Knot one end of each tube.

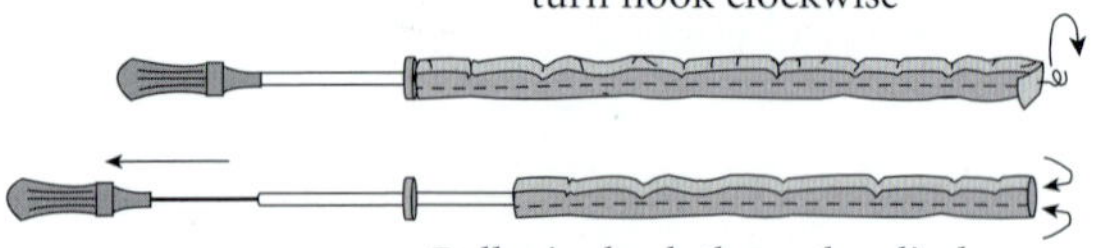

  - Position ties at upper edges of the tree skirt. Pin or baste in place.

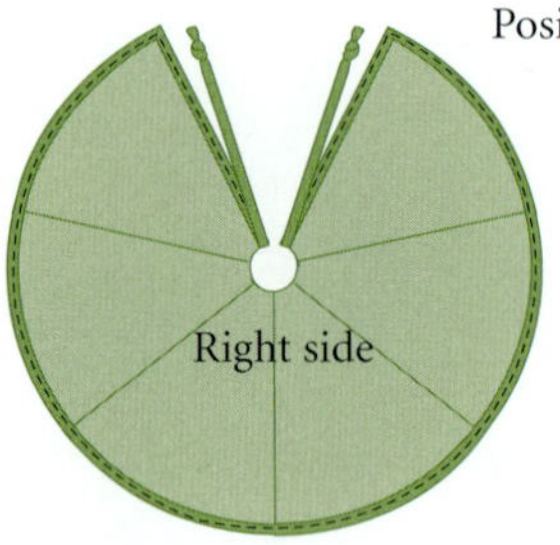

• Join lining to tree skirt.
  - Meet lining to tree skirt, right sides together. Keep loose ends of ties free from the stitching line. Stitch along center curved edge, sewing from cut edge to cut edge. Clip curve.

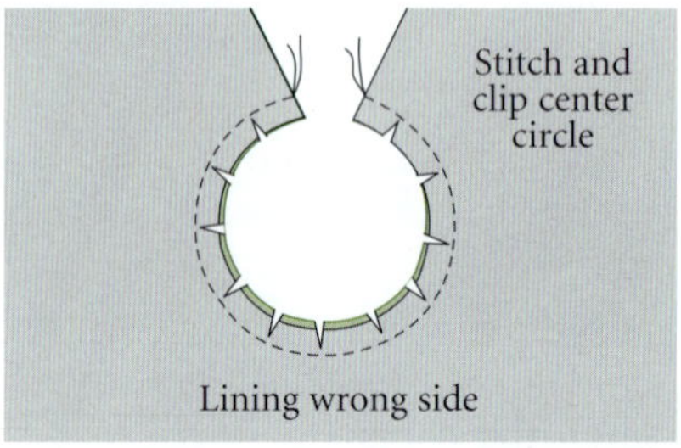

  - Press seam flat; then wrap seam toward the inside of the tree skirt, folding along the stitching line.
  - Stitch the adjoining straight edge of the skirt, beginning at the folded edge, continuing around the lower edge of the skirt, and leaving an opening on the final straight edge for turning. Press seam.

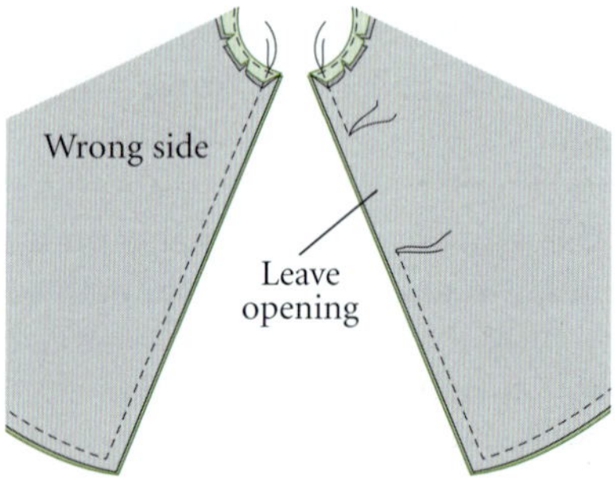

  - Notch outer edge; angle-cut corners. Press tree skirt flat.

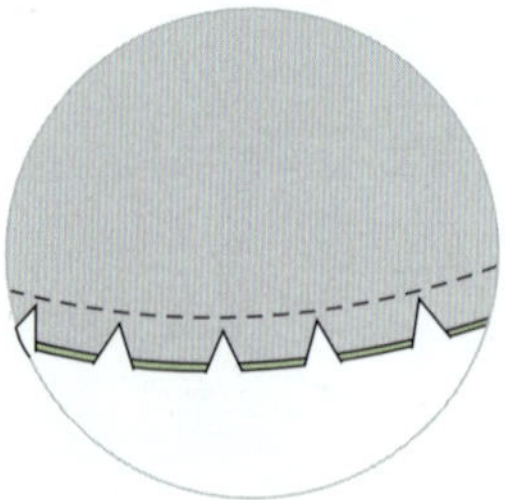

• Turn skirt right side out, using the Bamboo Pointer & Creaser to smooth the edges. Press edges and hand stitch opening closed.

Combining Designs to Make a Dimensional Wall Hanging

Using the same Amazing Designs® "Memories of Christmas" Memory Card, Eileen combined the Christmas motifs in this dimensional wall hanging. The scene has depth and dimension because the larger designs are in the foreground and the smaller designs are in the background.

1. Establish a horizon line for the design. Use sky-type fabric for the upper portion of the design and a cream-colored fabric for the lower snow area.

2. Position the design elements, again working from the background to the foreground.
3. Use quilting stitches to make a road to draw the eye up into the scene.
4. Add machine stitching to simulate snow drifts around the snowmen.

Add machine stitched snow drifts

Combining Machine Embroidery with Iron-on Transfers

Embroidery can easily be combined with other design elements such as iron-on transfers. (Bird•Scape, an iron-on transfer and embroidery disk project from Embroideryscapes™, was the starting point for the pictured design, also shown on the back cover.) Use a custom-sewn garment to showcase the design, or use a purchased garment. Either way, determining the position for the embroidery and transfers is critical.

1. Establish the position for the iron-on transfer.
   - With a ready-made garment, try on the garment to ensure proper placement.
   - With a constructed garment, stitch shoulder seams and try on the garment to determine positioning.

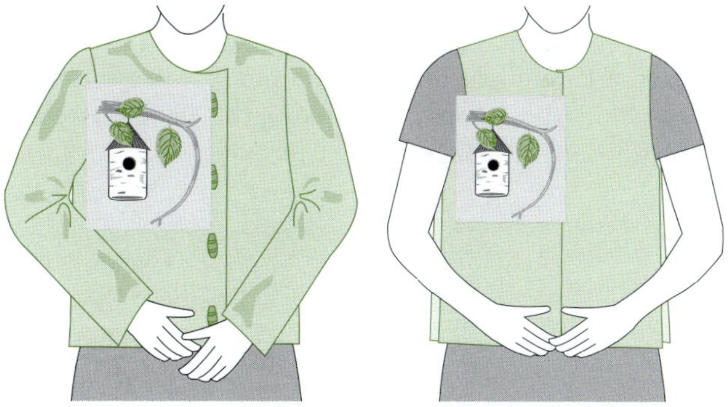

2. Position the transfer on the garment, meeting right sides. Press to transfer the design to the garment.
3. Use commercial templates or a stitched sample to position the embroidery designs.
   - It's always important to work from background to foreground.
   - Place the template over the transfer to indicate the position for embroidery stitching.
   - After positioning the design, hoop the fabric, align the machine needle with the hole in the template, remove the template, and stitch.
   - Create dimension by stitching portions of some elements over others.

Stitch portions of some elements over others

Adding Embroidery to Sweaters

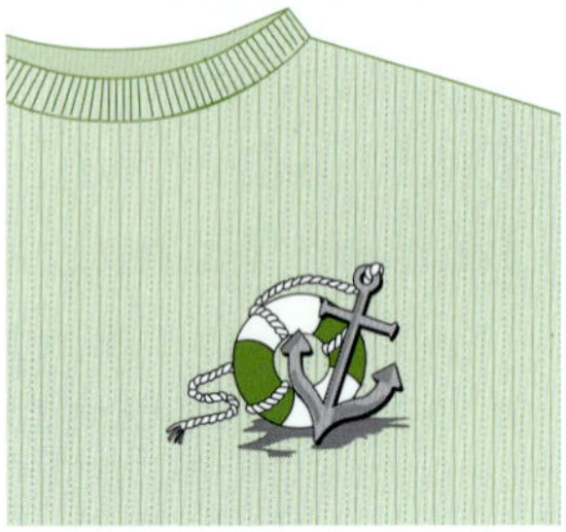

Duplicate the look of ready to wear by adding an embroidered design or monogram to a sweater. (Pictured design from Amazing Designs® "Memories by the Shore" Memory Card) Selecting and combining appropriate stabilizers is the key to stitching success.

1. Try on the garment; determine design placement and tape the template to the garment.
2. Select and apply stabilizers.
   - Press Totally Stable to the wrong side of the sweater. This temporarily prevents the knit from stretching.

   - Insert Filmoplast Stic in the hoop. Score the paper within the hoop and remove the paper covering, exposing the adhesive.

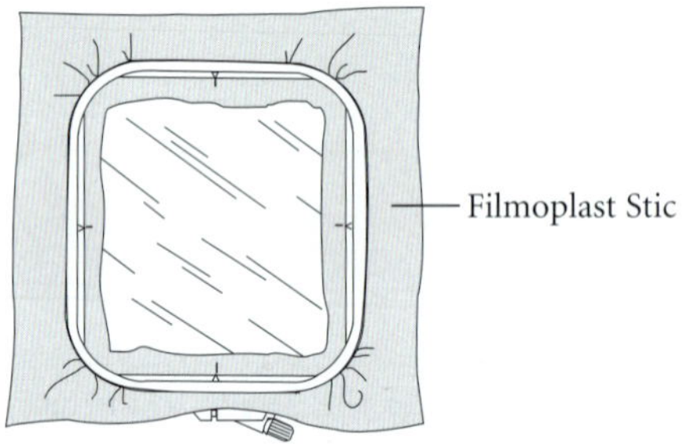

   - Position and hand-press the sweater over the Filmoplast adhesive.
   - Spray Avalon® with a fabric adhesive such as Sulky® KK2000™. Place the Avalon® over the area to be embroidered. This top stabilizer prevents the stitching from being embedded into the nap of the knit.

Always spray the stabilizer with the adhesive, rather than spraying the adhesive onto the garment. This prevents the garment from being saturated and makes it easier to remove the stabilizer and adhesive after stitching is completed.

Nancy

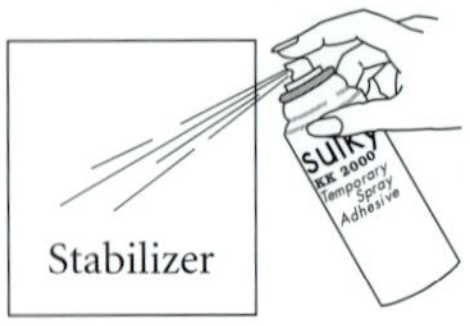

   - Insert the hoop in the sewing machine. There is no quick or easy way to do this. Maneuver the fabric to make sure the sweater fabric is flat and secure in the hoop and that the other layers of the sweater are out of the way.
   - Add a layer of cutaway stabilizer under the hoop.
   - Move the needle into correct position. Remove the template, lower the presser foot, and stitch.
   - Support the weight of the sweater with your hands to prevent the design from being distorted. Stay by the machine to ensure the remaining sweater fabric does not slip back into the sewing field.

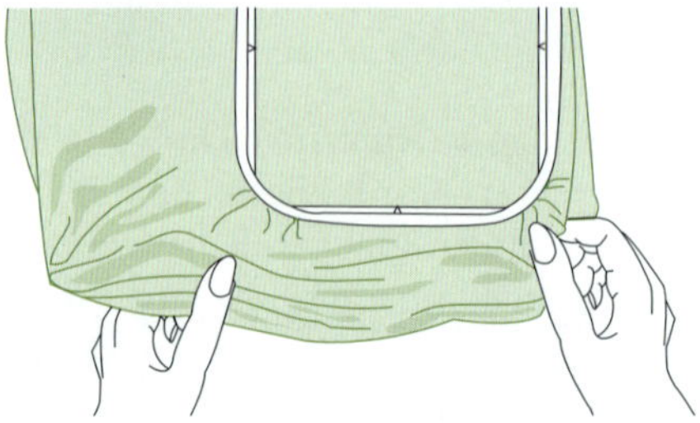

   - After stitching is completed, remove all the stabilizers.

High Tech Machine Embroidery

Next, take a look at how a computer and a sewing machine can "talk" to each other. Although not everyone has a sewing machine which has this capability, it's exciting to see what's available, how technology has changed, and how these developments allow us to be increasingly creative with our machines.

Many software programs are available for your personal computer, each designed for a specific purpose. One may help plan your budget; another may create greeting cards; a third may organize your family tree.

The same is true for software designed to work with machine embroidery. One may size and edit designs; another may incorporate and manipulate text. Each can help expand your creative embroidery options.

1. Install a reader/writer program on your computer. This program will be sewing machine specific. Some sewing machines can communicate directly with the computer, while others will need to have this separate software program installed on the computer hard drive.
2. Transfer the embroidery designs from disk or CD to a personal memory card.
   - Insert the disk or CD containing the embroidery designs into the computer.

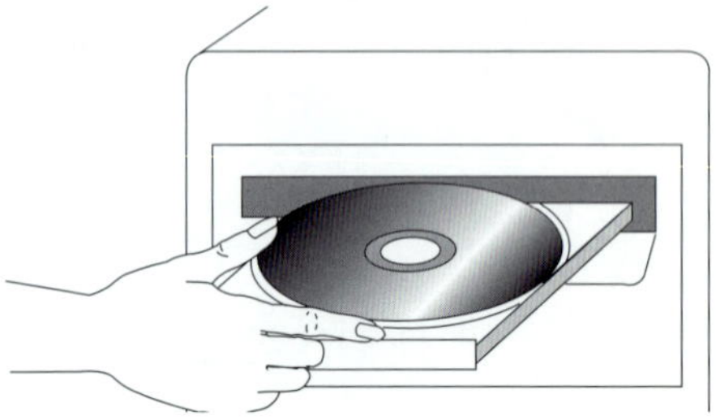

- Copy the designs to the hard drive.
- Open the reader/writer program.
- Open the design file.

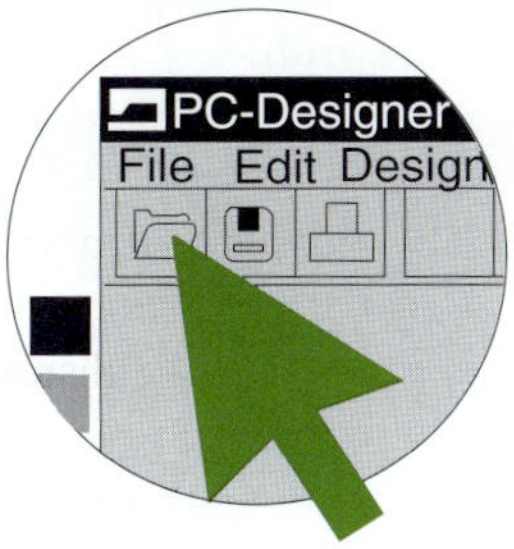

- Select the desired design. The design may appear in different colors than indicated on the disk literature. Don't worry. You can identify the colors you want when you stitch.
- Transfer the design to your personal memory card. This may take some time; have patience. On the sewing machine screen you will see graphics of both the computer and the sewing machine, with a line connecting the two to indicate they are communicating. When that line disappears, the transfer has been completed.

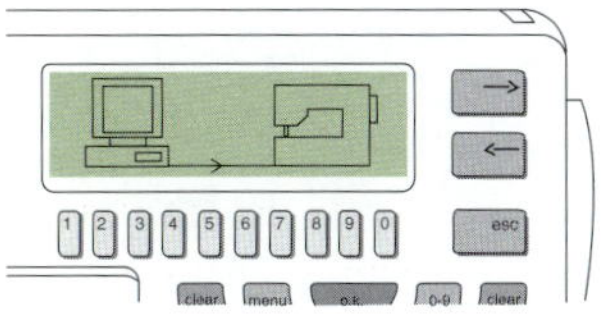

Transferring to memory card

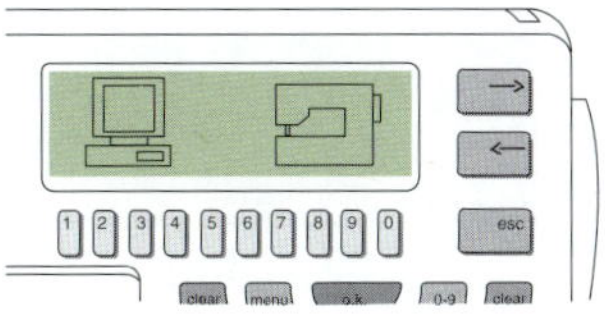

Transfer complete

Using a Sizing and Editing Program

Sizing and editing software offers incredible options. Delete portions or colors of a design, change the size, mirror image, rotate—all are possible with software such as Smart•Sizer Gold. In addition, you can combine design modifications to create a vast collection of designs. Of course, these modifications are possible only if designs are digitized in a language that your machine software can interpret.

1. Install the sizing and editing software. Open the program.

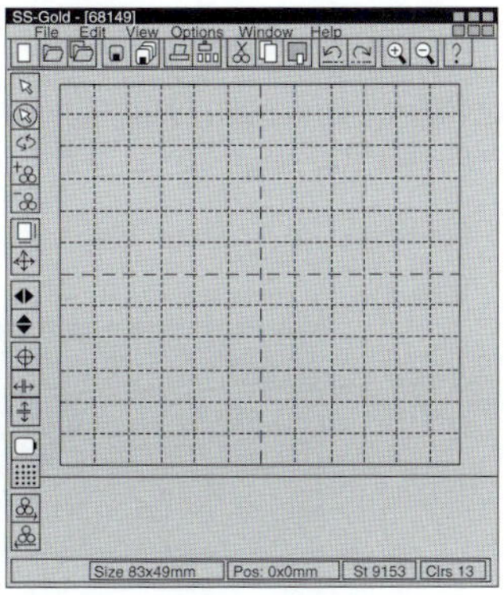

2. Choose and open a design from those copied to the hard drive.
3. Choose the appropriate hoop size.

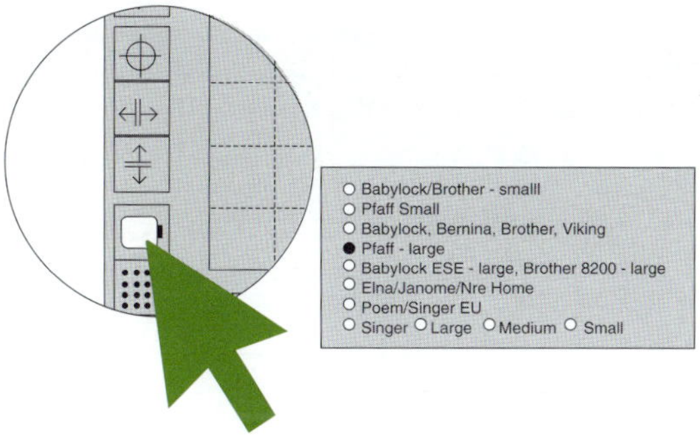

4. Change the color sequence or delete a color from the design.
   - Select the design. Handles appear around the entire design to indicate all portions have been selected.

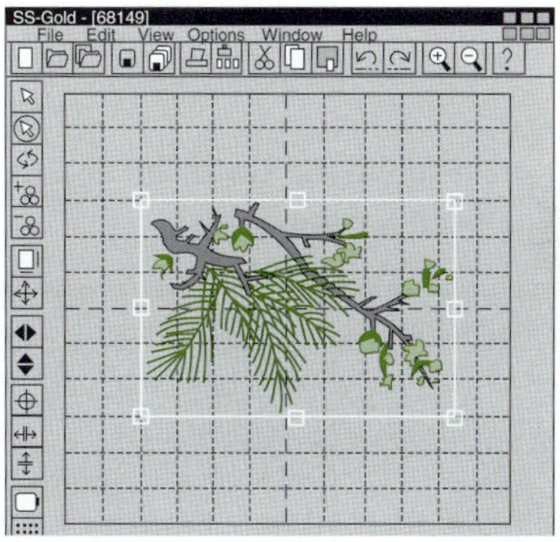

Select the design (pictured branch is from Amazing Designs® AD1095 Asian Home Decor Collection I)

   - Select "Search/select colors." This allows you to go through the design color by color so you can identify what gets stitched at one time with a particular color.
   - Select the "Color" tool. Highlight the color you wish to delete. Hit "Delete" and that portion of the design is gone. Save the modified design and transfer it to your personal memory card using a read/write program. Then sew.

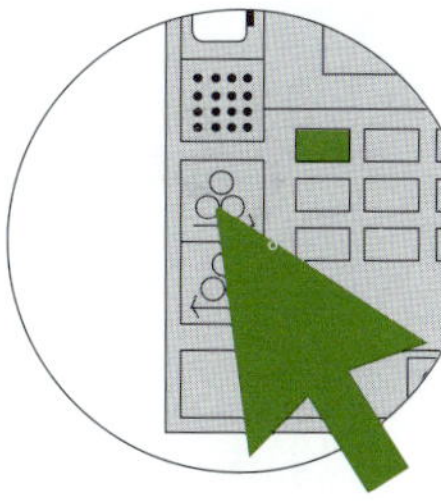

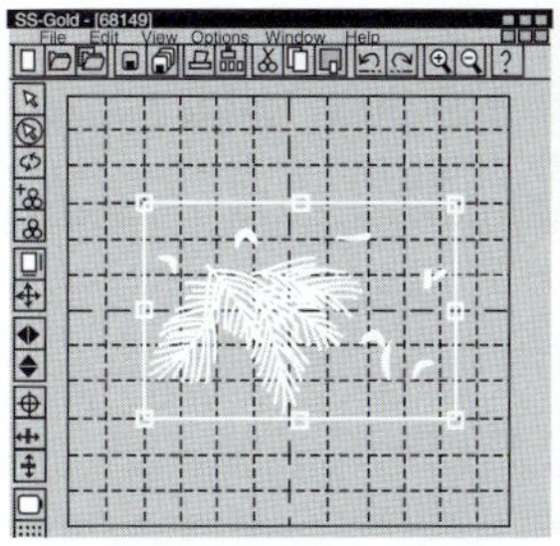

Highlight color

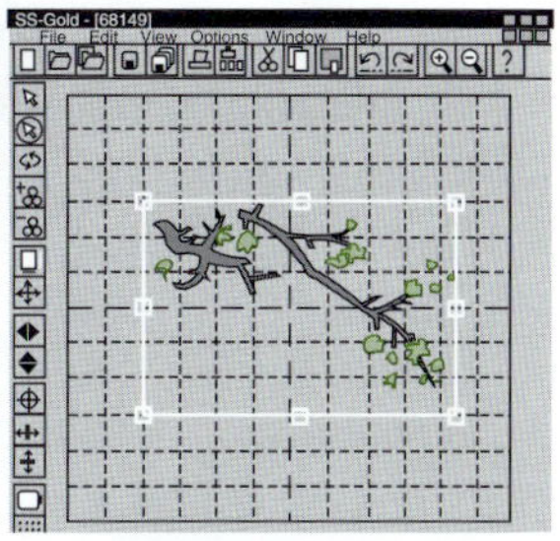

Design with color deleted

5. Personalize a design by mirror-imaging the design, changing its size, or changing stitch density.
   - Select the entire design.
   - Mirror image the design horizontally or vertically.

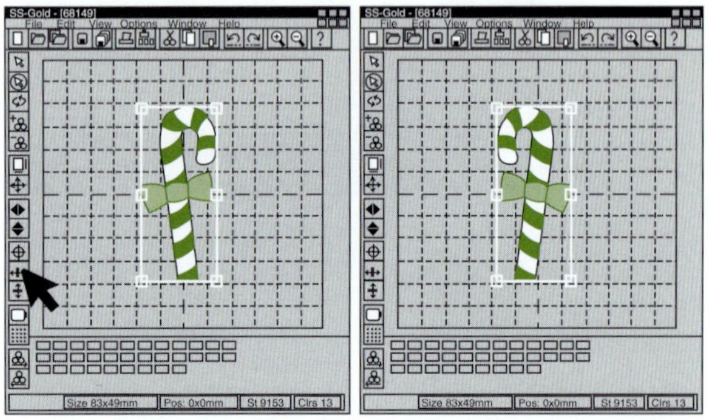

Select design — Mirror image design

(Pictured design is part of Amazing Designs® AD1097, Holiday Pocket Toppers Collection I disk pack)

   - Save the modified design, adding the suffix "MI" to indicate the design has been mirror imaged.

6. Personalize a design by changing its size.
   - Select the original design.
     - Grab one of the handles on the design and drag to enlarge or reduce the design.

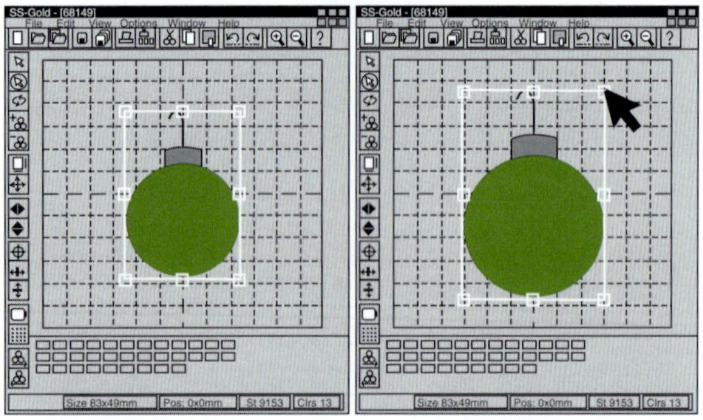

Select design — Drag handle to enlarge

(Pictured design is part of Amazing Designs® AD1097, Holiday Pocket Toppers Collection I disk pack)

     - Save the modified design, adding an identifying suffix to indicate the design has been enlarged or reduced.

7. Personalize a design by changing the stitch density.
   - Select the "density" tool.
   - Several choices will appear (for example, 60 wt., 40 wt., and yarn). The default is 40 wt. thread.
   - By selecting "yarn," stitches will be farther apart.

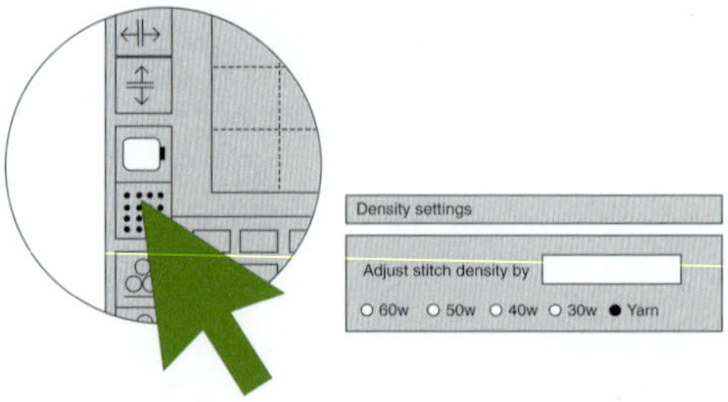

   - Save the modified design, adding an identifying suffix to indicate the design has been modified.
   - On the project pictured below, Eileen positioned fabric over the fish design and stitched over the fabric. By modifying the thread selection, stitches will become more or less dense, allowing less or more of the background fabric to be visible.

(Pictured design from Amazing Designs® AD1125, Tropical Fish Collection I disk pack)

8. Manipulate a design by rotating it.
   - Open the sizing and editing program.
   - Select the "rotation" tool.
   - Grab one handle; rotate it desired number of degrees.

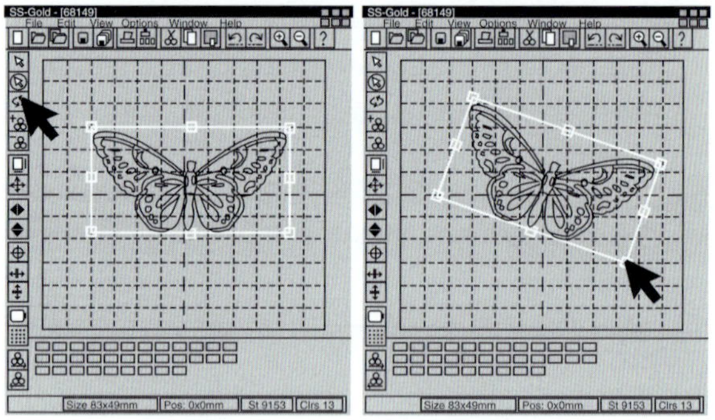

Select design — Grab handle to rotate

(Pictured design from Amazing Designs® AD1014, Butterfly Collection I)

   - Save the modified design, adding an identifying suffix to indicate the design has been modified.

Using a Lettering Program

Text programs such as Lettering Pro allow you to personalize projects by adding embroidered names, monograms, or text of your choice. In addition, you can combine text with other embroidery designs for added impact and interest.

1. Open the lettering program. Select the hoop size.

2. Use the stock lettering tool and enter desired text. Text will appear on a single line until a "return" is entered.

3. To add a second line of text, insert a "return" after the first line.

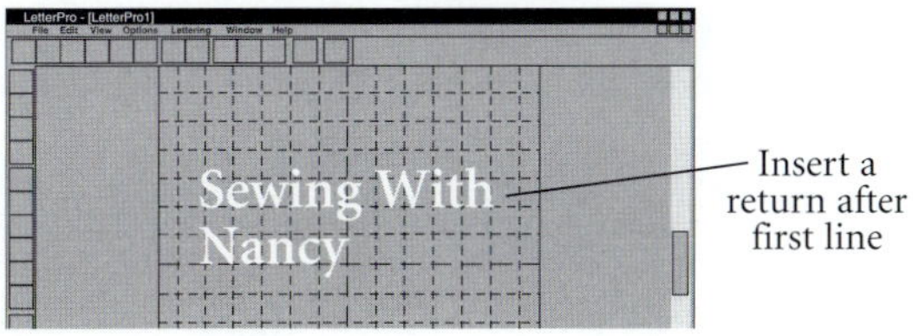

4. Modify the text as desired.
   - Change text size.
     - Each pictured box indicates one of the letters in the text. Left click to see the actual letters. To change the size of all the text, select all the text and use the up and down arrows.
     - To change the size of one letter, right click on only that letter. An "X" will appear in the selected letter. A message at the lower edge of the screen indicates the size.

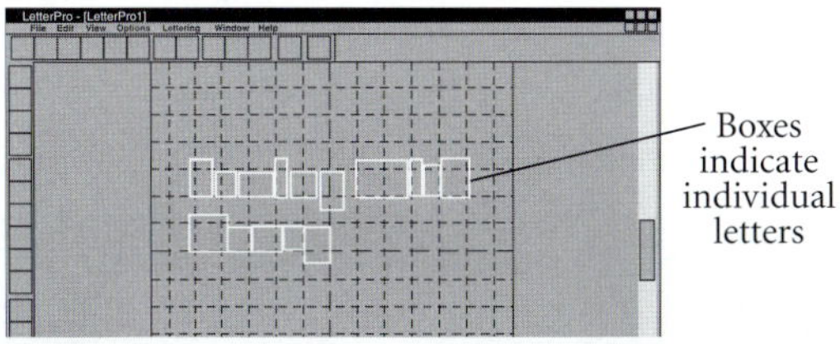

   - Change the font of an individual letter, a whole word, or the entire line of text.

5. Combine text with an embroidery design.
   - Open the embroidery design.

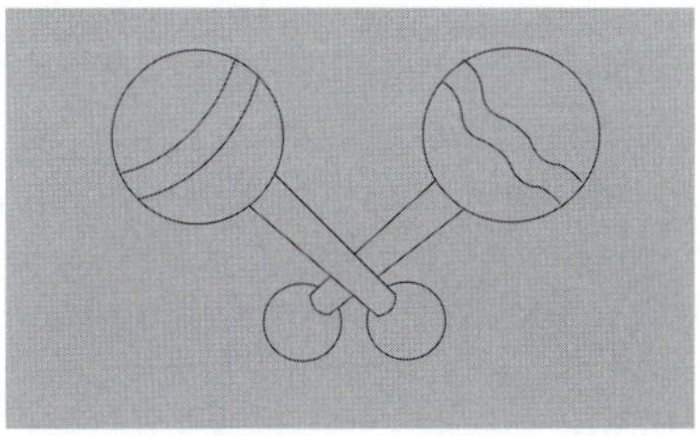

(Pictured design from Amazing Designs® AD1098, Baby Bibs Collection I)

   - Open the lettering program and add text as detailed above.

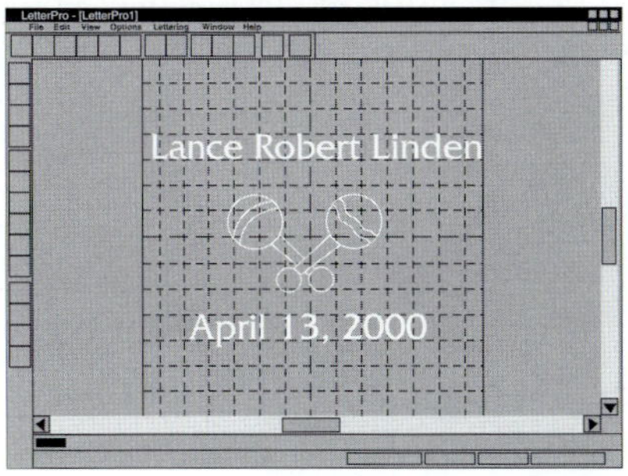

   - If desired, manipulate the text by arcing the text.
     - Select the "arc" tool.

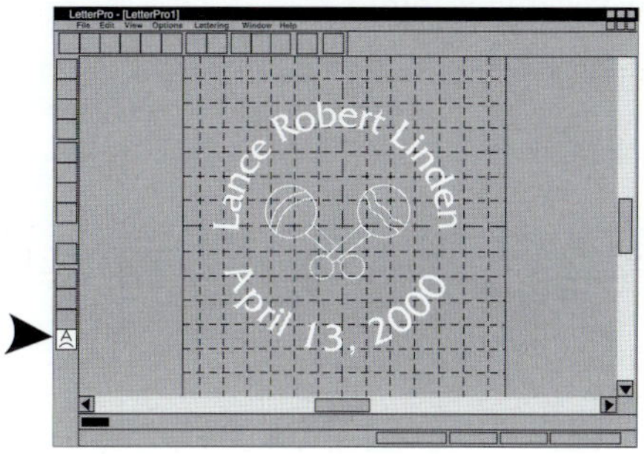

     - Adjust the arc if necessary.
     - Go back to the stock lettering tool to turn the lettering into stitches.

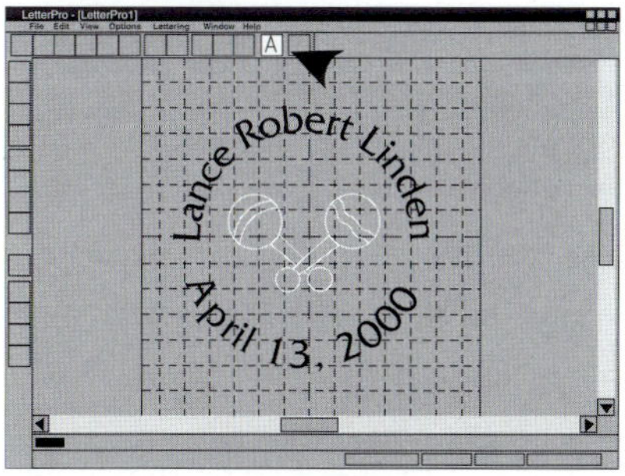

     - Save and transfer the design to a memory card using a read/write program.
     - Stitch out the design.

Downloading Designs from the Internet

In addition to embroidery designs available for purchase on memory cards, disks, and CDs, free embroidery designs are also available from a number of sources. If you have Internet access, you'll find designs which can be downloaded to your computer. (Naturally, you'll need a reader/writer program or a converter box so your computer can communicate with your sewing machine.) On our *Sewing With Nancy®* web site, we've posted a free design which can be used either as an outline design or an appliqué design. Here's how to download that design.

1. Insert a personal memory card for your sewing machine in the machine or converter box.

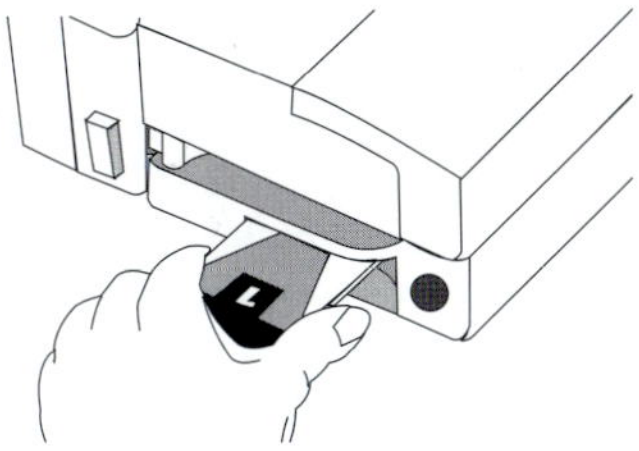

2. Open your Internet connection.

   Go to www.sewingwithnancy.com

http://www.sewingwithnancy.com

3. Click on "Sewing Room."

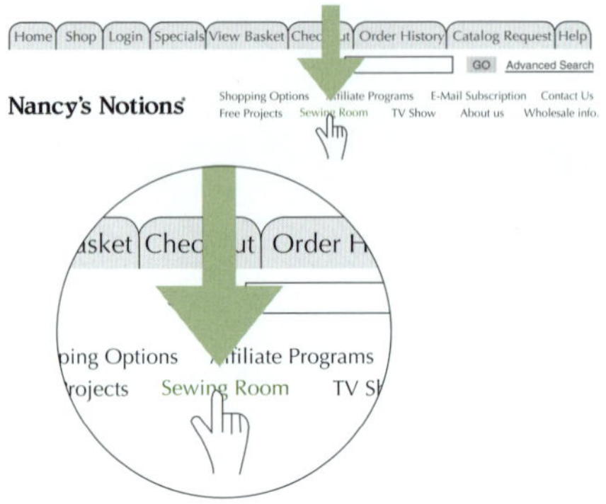

4. Click on "Free embroidery design."

5. Download that design to your computer; then transfer it to your memory card as detailed on pages 12–13, and you're ready to stitch.

Making an Evening Bag

This attractive evening bag showcases the free machine embroidery design which is available at our web site. With a small investment of time and embroidery stitching, you'll have an elegant evening bag. Finished size: approximately 7" x 8½" (28 cm x 21.8 cm).

Supplies needed:

- ⅓ yd. (0.3 m) fashion fabric
- ⅓ yd. (0.3 m) lining fabric
- ⅓ yd. (0.3 m) fusible interfacing
- Filmoplast Stic Stabilizer
- Tear-away stabilizer
- Machine Embroidery Thread

Making the Bag

1. Download the design to a personal memory card as detailed above. Modify the design by changing the three colors to "mono" so the design stitches continuously in one color. Save the modified design on the memory card.

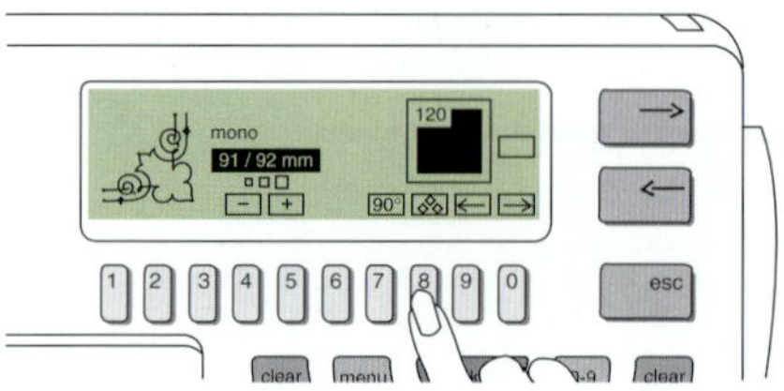

Select mono

2. Make the pattern for the evening bag.
   - Trace and cut out the flap pattern on page 18 onto Pattern Paper, including the position points and notches.
   - Add 14" (35.5 cm) length to the flap pattern.

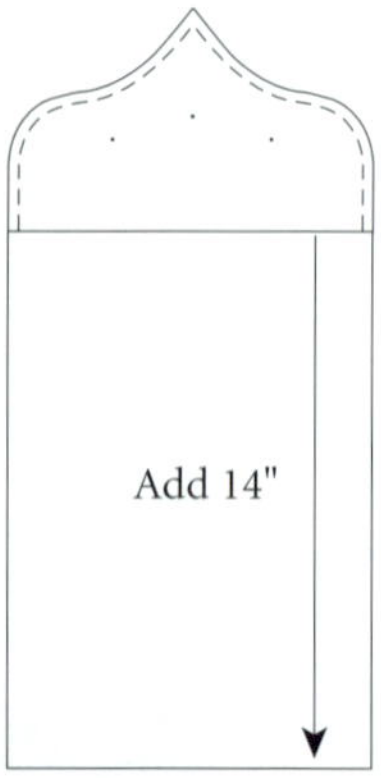

3. Prepare the fabric and embroider the flap.
   - Fuse interfacing to the wrong side of the fashion fabric.
   - Transfer cutting lines, position points, and notches to the right side of the fabric.

   - Hoop the fabric. Be sure the fabric is taut. (If the fashion fabric has a napped surface or hooping would leave an imprint on the fabric, insert Filmoplast Stic Stabilizer in the hoop, gridded side up. Score and remove the protective paper, exposing the adhesive. Then adhere the fabric to the Filmoplast.)
     - Stitch out the design on a test fabric to serve as a positioning guide. (See page 5.)
     - Using the stitched design as a template, align the fabric in the hoop (or position it over the adhesive and pat the fabric in place), aligning marked horizontal and vertical center marks and top of design.

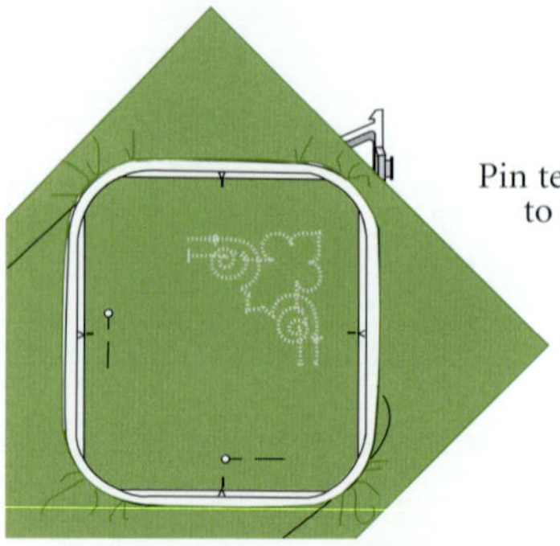

Pin test design to fabric

     - Attach the hoop to the embroidery unit. Position the needle to align with the marked center. Then remove the stitched placement guide.

- Slip a piece of tear-away stabilizer under the hoop. Embroider the design.

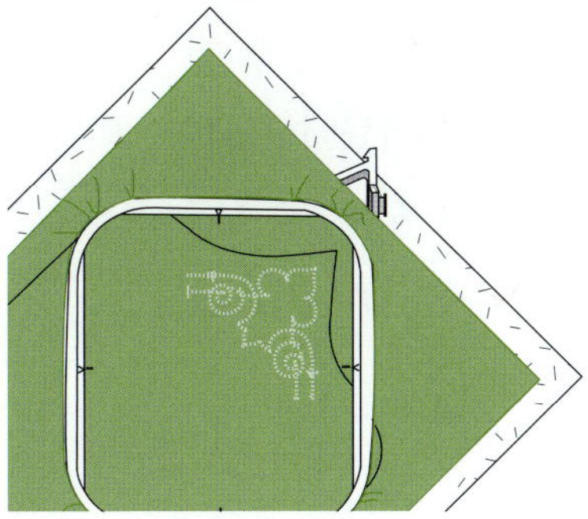

- Repeat, rehooping and repositioning the template for the two remaining portions of the design.
- Remove excess stabilizer when stitching is completed.

4. Assemble the bag.
   - Cut out the evening bag and lining along the traced edge. Trim 1/8" (0.3 cm) from the short straight end of the lining. This helps prevent the lining from showing on the outside of the bag.

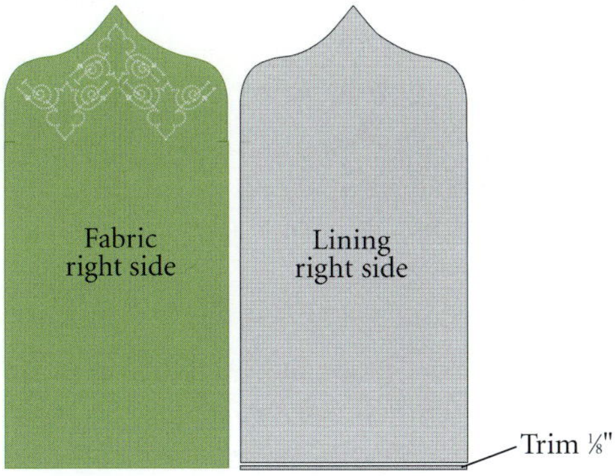

   - Meet lining to evening bag, right sides together. Stitch along curved flap edge, starting and ending at notches. Also stitch along opposite short edge.

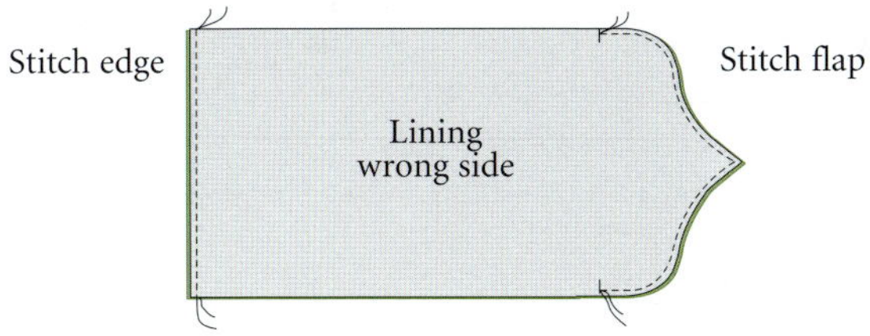

   - Clip and notch curved edge. Clip to stitching line at flap notch.

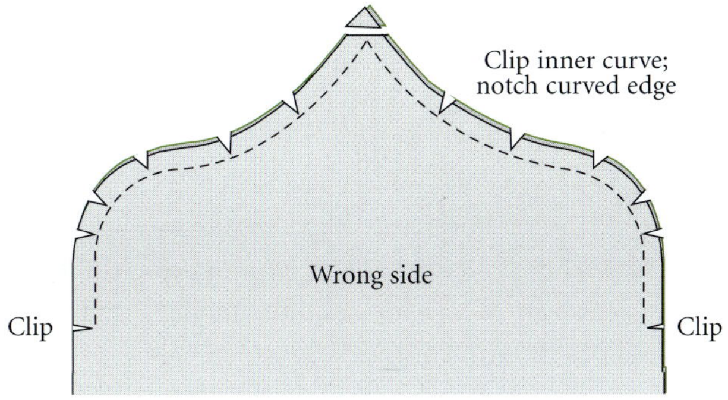

- Press seam on short end toward lining. Understitch seam.

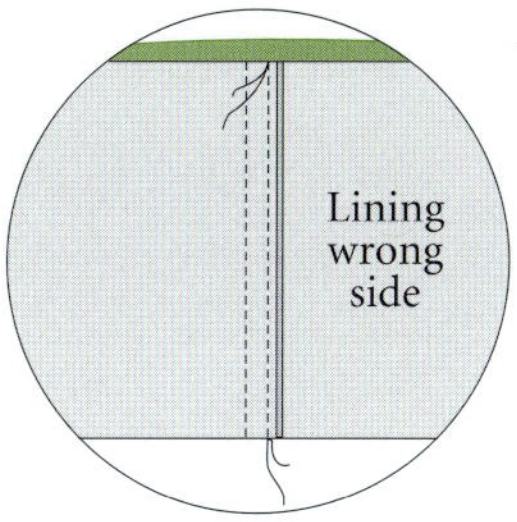

- Turn bag right side out. Press both stitched edges.
- Stitch side seams.
  - Meet understitched edge to flap notches, right sides together, aligning cut edges. Stitch sides with 1/4" (0.6 cm) seams.

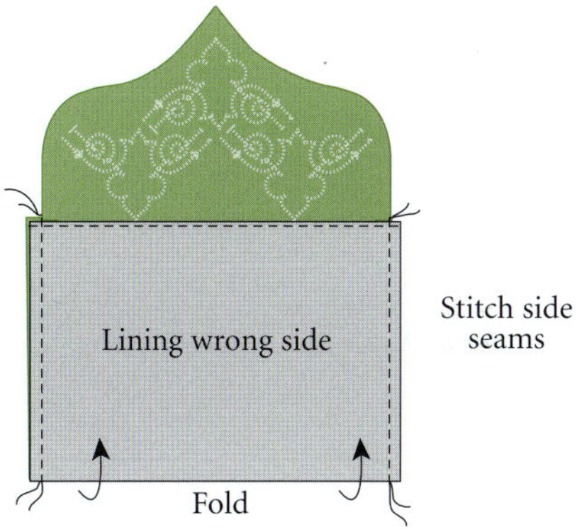

  - Serge or zigzag seam to prevent raveling.

- Miter lower corners.
  - Fold the lower edge so the side seam is stacked on top of the lower fold, forming a triangle.
  - Stitch perpendicular to the seam 1" (2.5 cm) from the point, reinforcing stitching at each end.

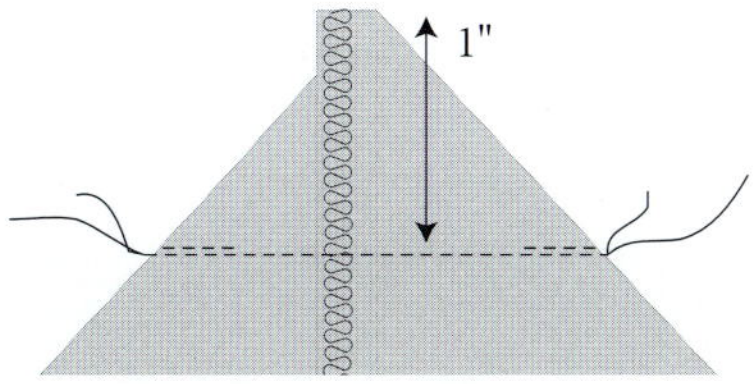

- Turn bag right side out.
- Optional: Add cording straps.

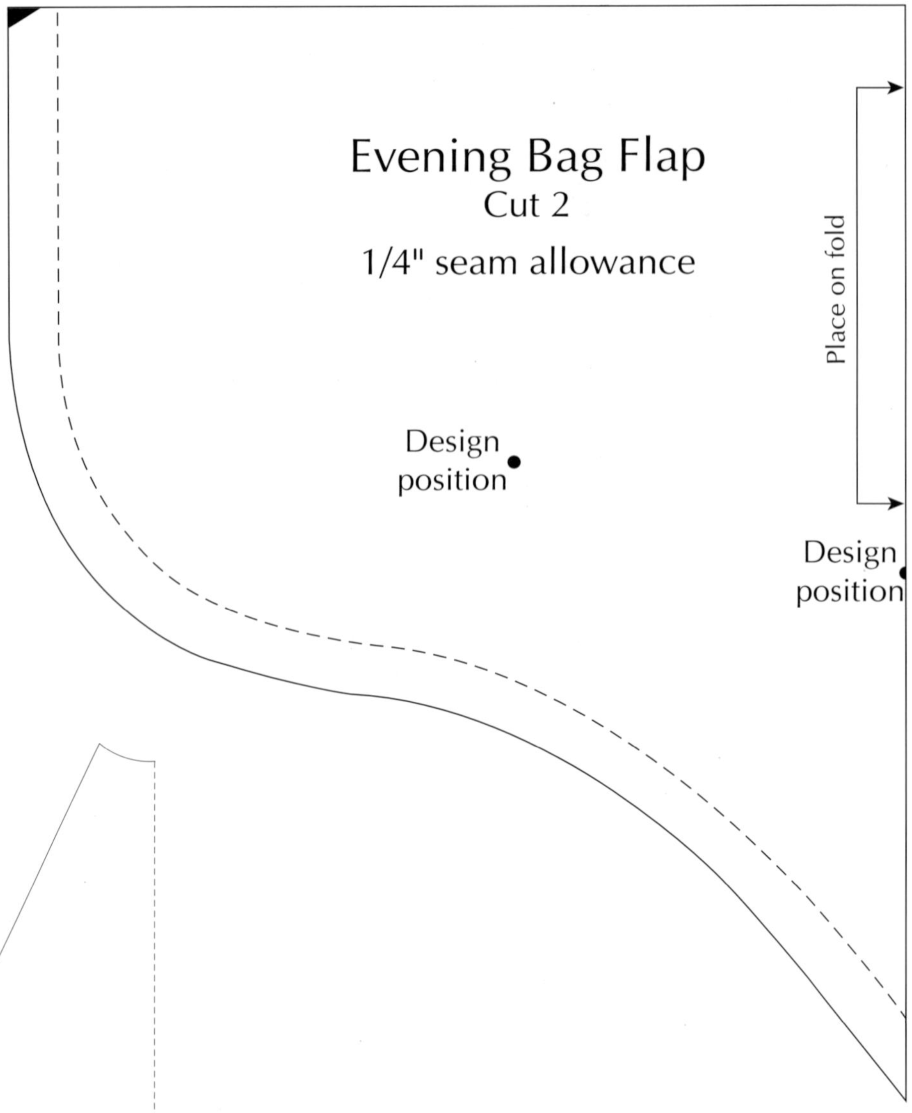
Evening Bag Flap
Cut 2
1/4" seam allowance
Place on fold
Design position
Design position

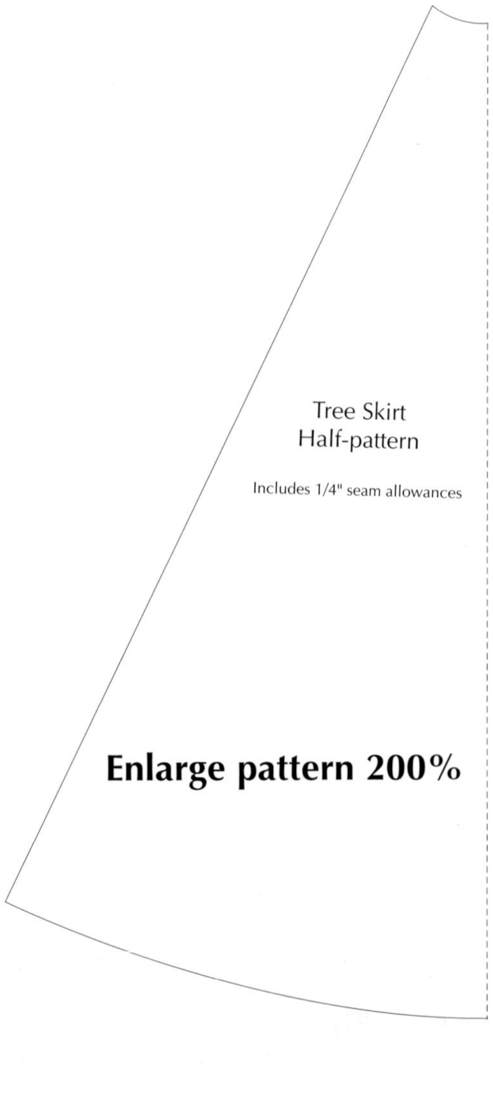
Tree Skirt
Half-pattern
Includes 1/4" seam allowances
Enlarge pattern 200%